# ELIZABETH RING

# RANCH AND FARM DOGS

## HERDERS
## AND GUARDS

GOOD DOGS!
THE MILLBROOK PRESS ▪ BROOKFIELD, CONNECTICUT

**FOR JEAN, ELAINE, VICKY, AND MARY ELLEN:
GOOD GIRLS!**

Cover photo courtesy of Elaine Pascoe
Photos courtesy of R. Coppinger, Hampshire College: pp. 3, 21,
24; The Ranch Dog Trainer: pp. 4 (courtesy Barbara Klein), 12
(courtesy Judith Kelly), 19 (courtesy Mary Nouwens), 23 (courtesy Mary Nouwens); UPI/Bettmann: pp. 6, 13; Bill Hennefrund:
pp. 8, 9; Kent & Donna Dannen: pp. 17, 28; Roger A. Woodruff,
USDA-Aphis: p. 22; Jim McEwen: p. 27.

Library of Congress Cataloging-in-Publication Data
Ring, Elizabeth, 1920–
Ranch and farm dogs: herders and guards / by Elizabeth Ring.
p.   cm.—(Good dogs!)
Includes bibliographical references (p.     ) and index.
Summary: Highlights Border collies, Welsh corgis, and
Great Pyrenees sheepdogs and describes their charac-
teristics, training, and typical days at work and play.
ISBN 1-56294-295-6 (lib. bdg.)
1. Herding dogs—Juvenile literature.   2. Livestock protection
dogs—Juvenile literature.   [1. Working dogs.   2. Dogs.]
I. Title.   II. Series: Ring, Elizabeth, 1920–   Good dogs!
SF428.6.R56   1994   636.7'0886—dc20
93-41529   CIP   AC

Published by The Millbrook Press
2 Old New Milford Road
Brookfield, Connecticut 06804

# RANCH AND FARM DOGS

Border collies, probably the favorite dog of farmers and ranchers,
are known for their intelligence and alert response to commands.

One summer day in Scotland, two frisky lambs broke out of a sheep pen. Kicking their heels, they dashed up the hill toward a large flock of sheep where their mothers grazed. Instantly, Nell, a black-and-white Border collie, took off after them.

Halfway up the hill the lambs split, one going this way, one that. Nell, a born sheepherder and the boss of "her" flock, quickly got one lamb turned around and back into the pen.

By then, lamb number two had disappeared among about four hundred sheep. Even so, without orders from anyone, Nell wove her way through the flock, located the lamb, and backed it against a fence. Crouching close to the ground, Nell stared at the lamb as if daring it to make a move. Every time the lamb did try to dart past her, Nell blocked the way. Determinedly, she kept the skittish animal pinned to the spot until her shepherd came to take over.

"That'll do!" said the shepherd, giving his dog a quick pat.

Nell relaxed and trotted at the shepherd's side as he led the lamb back to the pen. Then she stood by, ready for the next game of "go get the sheep."

**HERDERS AND GUARDS IN HISTORY** ▪ Dogs have been helping to tend people's flocks and herds since before people knew how to raise animals for food.

Long, long ago, scientists guess, people made friends with wolves (and possibly jackals)—the ancestors of dogs. At first

A shepherd and his best friend share a snack on a Montana sheep ranch in this photograph taken in the late nineteenth century. The shepherd, alone on the plains with his flock, depended on his dog to guard and control the sheep.

they probably worked as partners in hunting wild animals and fighting off fierce wild beasts. Hundreds of years later, dogs and people were still partners, now guiding and protecting tamed herds and flocks. Some animals were shepherded from open pasture to open pasture; some were grazed on fenced-in ranges and farms.

Generation after generation, dogs were bred to herd and guard—but not to harm—the animals they tended. In time, the dogs lost their instinct to kill but kept their strong instinct to track and capture animals. That made them good herders. And the dogs' instinct to protect their own territories made them good guards. In return, people fed and cared for their dogs.

Over the years, wherever there have been large bands of reindeer, sheep, cows, and other domesticated animals, there have been dogs to take care of them. Dogs have worked in the mountains and pastures of Europe, Asia, Africa, Australia, New Zealand, and North and South America.

In the United States, dogs have worked as herders and guards on farms and ranches from Maine to California. As guards, they have proved to be more efficient than electric fences and noise machines, and less cruel than poisons and traps in saving livestock from predators (such as coyotes and bears).

On some farms, one dog both herds and guards animals. On most farms, however, dogs are ''specialists,'' either herding or guarding.

Today, many dogs bred to herd and guard live in homes as pets. Without livestock to tend, herding dogs try to herd people,

# Sheepdog Training Commands

| | |
|---|---|
| *"Come"* | Come to wherever I am standing. |
| *"Come by"* | Move out to the far side of the flock, circling clockwise to the animals' left. |
| *"Way to me"* | Move out to the far side of the flock, circling counterclockwise to the animals' right. |
| *"Down"* | Lie down immediately, on the spot. Face the flock quietly, fixing them with a stare. |
| *"Come on"* | Move close to the flock. |
| *"Go back"* | Move away from the flock. |
| *"Hup"* | Speed up. |
| *"That'll do"* | Stop working and come to me. |

cars, tennis balls—or even scraps of paper. As pets, guarding dogs often fiercely insist on protecting their families and property—which can sometimes make visitors feel unwelcome!

**HERDING DOGS** ▪ Herding dogs work with sheep, cattle, goats, ducks, geese, chickens, and other livestock. Some dogs work with only one kind of animal; other dogs might herd two kinds —such as cattle and sheep or sheep and goats.

A Welsh corgi gets its ducks in a row at a herding instinct test in Colorado. This kind of competition gives dogs a chance to show off their skills.

# Traditional Header Breeds

**The Australian Kelpie** (Scottish for "little helper") is probably a mix of Welsh and Scottish sheep-dogs (including the collie) plus some Australian dingo (wild dog). Tireless, even in intense heat, it is the most common sheepdog in Australia and New Zealand. It is famous for its skill in keeping sheep together by pushing them with its shoulders and head.

**The Australian Shepherd** (or "Aussie") is a smart, courageous dog that may have Border collie blood. A versatile dog that is header, heeler, and guard of sheep and cattle, it was, despite its name, developed in America.

**The Bearded Collie** is a Scottish breed that, except for its unbobbed tail, looks like a lighter-bodied Old English sheepdog and has many of the herding qualities of a Border collie.

**The Border Collie** (also called "shepherd's collie" or "English collie") is named for the border between England and Scotland. It is a cross of several breeds, including the collie, which historians believe was brought to the British Isles by the Romans, who also brought sheep from Spain.

**The Collie** (possibly for "coal-y" because of the black color of the dog's ancestors, or for "coelio," Welsh for "to trust"), both rough-coated (like "Lassie") and smooth, is from Scotland. The rough-coated collie became a favorite of Queen Victoria in the mid-nineteenth century.

**The Shetland Sheepdog** (or "Sheltie") comes from the Shetland Islands, which are known for their miniature sheepdogs, ponies, and sheep. The dog is most likely a descendant of the Scottish collie.

Different breeds of herding dogs are divided into two kinds: "headers" and "heelers." While some herding dogs are both headers and heelers, most are one or the other.

Headers, such as Border collies and Shetland sheepdogs, work at the animals' heads to steer them in one direction or another. Heelers (also called "drovers"), such as Welsh corgis and Australian cattle dogs, drive animals forward by following after them, sometimes nipping and barking at the animals' heels.

**THE WORK OF HEADERS ▪** Several breeds of dogs work as headers, and each breed has its special qualities. They are hardworking dogs that spend hours running over rocks and fields, through forests and swamps, searching for flocks and herds, rounding them up, and herding them home.

Border collies are, by far, favorites as "heading" dogs, especially on sheep farms. These tough dogs have working abilities that few other breeds have.

A Border collie has a stalking style all its own. It crouches close to the ground as it approaches a flock, moving quietly and steadily—not so close as to frighten the sheep but not so far away as to escape their attention.

A Border collie's key quality is its "eye" (a hard stare). When a Border collie fixes its eye on sheep, the sheep seem to feel hypnotized—as if they are in the dog's power.

A Border collie like Nell has a busy year on a sheep farm. Summer is "dipping" and "shearing" time. During dipping time, sheep are brought in from the fields and dunked in troughs of "sheep-dip" to get rid of ticks, lice, and fleas. When sheep are sheared, Nell helps bring the ewes (female sheep) in from the fields to have their wool clipped. One of Nell's jobs is to help separate the lambs from the ewes and keep the lambs under control. Later, she gets lambs and ewes back together, and later still, she helps get the lambs off to market, herding them onto trucks.

The Border collie takes its job very seriously, although this little lamb doesn't look too hard to control.

The Australian kelpie stops at nothing to get a job done—
including running across sheep's backs to get past a flock.

Fall is even busier for Nell. This is ''tupping'' time. The tups (male sheep) are mated with the ewes so that more lambs will be born the following spring. Again, it is Nell's job to gather the ewes into paddocks or pens.

Winter can be a quiet time (in good weather) for sheep and dogs. Sheep spend most of their days roaming the pastures and hills, eating from feed blocks placed in the grassless fields.

But after a snowstorm, off Nell goes to locate the flock. Sometimes the sheep get buried deep in the snow, and Nell has to use her good scenting abilities to sniff them out.

Spring is ''lambing'' time — by far the busiest time of year on a sheep farm. Nell keeps the sheep sorted by shifting the ewes and lambs from pen to pen as the lambs are born.

**TRAINING OF HEADERS** ▪ In any working dog's first lessons, it learns to obey, in the same way that pet dogs are taught to ''come,'' ''sit,'' ''lie down,'' and ''stay.'' Training a dog to work as a header often begins by teaching the pup to herd small manageable ducks and chickens, not bigger or bolder animals such as sheep, goats, or cattle.

Later, a dog works with whatever animals it is being trained to herd. Some handlers use whistles and hand signals to direct dogs that are far out in a field.

**THE WORK OF HEELERS** ▪ At sundown on a large dairy farm in New Hampshire, Cap, a small, tireless Cardigan Welsh corgi,

# Traditional Heeler Breeds

**The Australian Cattle Dog** (or "Queensland blue heeler" or "Bluey"—for the blue-speckled coat of some dogs; others are red-speckled) is a tough, quick, steady dog, probably part collie, Dalmation, kelpie, and dingo (Australian wild dog). It is an excellent herder and protector.

**The Bernese Mountain Dog** (or "Swiss mountain dog"), named for Bern, Switzerland, is a big, mastifflike Swiss mountain dog that has been used to drive cattle, carry packs, pull carts, and guard livestock. The Bernese has a remarkable memory. It can, some say, recognize each animal in its herd.

**The Briard** (possibly named for its French home of Brie) is a shaggy herding and guard dog that resembles the Bearded collie and the Old English sheepdog.

**The Puli** (meaning "driver"), from Hungary, is a smaller, darker relative of the komondor, usually black or gray. In a pinch, a puli can ride the back of a runaway sheep until the sheep tires and stops running.

**The Rottweiler** (named for Rottweil, Germany) is a sturdy, hard-working dog that probably came to Europe as a cattle drover when the Romans crossed the Alps to invade Europe. In Germany these dogs herded cattle to market.

**The Welsh Corgi** (meaning a "dwarf dog" in Welsh—the corgi being the shortest of the herders) includes the Cardigan and the tailless Pembroke. They are long-bodied, short-legged dogs trained in Wales to work with cattle, sheep, hogs, and mountain ponies, and to hunt rabbits and kill vermin such as rats.

was driving a herd of cows in from pasture. He dashed this way and that behind the snuffling, mooing animals.

As a born heeler (or drover), it was second nature to Cap to drive livestock before him, and he did this every day—in the morning out to their grazing grounds, at night back to the barn.

That evening, most of the cows plodded along ahead of Cap. Only one stubborn cow hung back. Cap got behind her and barked. The cow turned and gazed at the dog, refusing to budge. Cap snapped at the cow's heels. The cow kicked. But, like most heelers, Cap was quick enough and small enough to duck. Cap did not give up. Tough and fearless, he kept nipping at the cow's hooves—and ducking the cow's kicks. Finally the cranky cow tossed her head and followed the rest of the herd. Cap kept a sharp eye out, ready to push any other stragglers back in line.

**TRAINING OF HEELERS** ▪ Training a dog to work as a ''heeler'' often begins (after basic obedience training) with a pup driving sheep, pigs, goats, or cattle down a narrow, fenced road where the animals cannot scatter. At first, some trainers themselves drive the slow-moving animals, getting a pup to follow. Other trainers let a pup work alongside an older, experienced dog. Most dogs bred as heelers do not need much training to nip at the animals' heels. They do it by instinct.

As a dog follows its animals, a handler might say ''hup 'em'' or ''drive on'' or ''move up'' and motion forward with an arm, staff, or stick. To keep a herd from turning off into a side road, a dog is sent forward to head off the animals at the turnoff.

This Border collie is learning to herd sheep. Here the trainer is commanding the dog to fetch the sheep to him.

A heeler must learn not to drive the animals too fast. With the dog at first on leash, the trainer repeats the word ''slow.'' It takes about a month for a well-bred heeler to be ready to work off leash on its own.

**GUARDING DOGS** ▪ It was lambing time on the Oregon sheep ranch where Jeff, a big white Great Pyrenees sheepdog, worked as a guarding dog. Late one afternoon, the rancher went out to check on his flock. How many new lambs had been born today?

# Traditional Guard Dog Breeds

**The Akbash** is a large, white dog from Turkey, said to be descended from mastiffs and swift, sharp-sighted sighthounds. It is known for its tendency to challenge intruders aggressively.

**The Anatolian Shepherd** is from Turkey, where it is still used to guard sheep. It is more aggressive than many other guard dogs. It is sometimes provided with a spiked collar for protection from wolves (or as a symbol of having beaten a wolf in a fight).

**The German Shepherd** dog's ancestors include several German working dogs. The German shepherd is well known for its intelligence, agility, scenting ability, and herding and guarding instincts.

**The Great Pyrenees,** largest of guard dogs, comes from the mountains along the border of France and Spain. Big, powerful, but gentle, it is descended from Tibetan mastiffs brought to Europe probably around 1800-1000 B.C.

**The Komondor** was brought from Asia to Hungary over a thousand years ago. As white and shaggy as a sheep, it blends with its flock. Its long, thick corded coat protects it from enemies and harsh weather.

**The Maremma,** for centuries a sheepdog in the mountains of Central Italy, is probably related to the Great Pyrenees.

**The Old English Sheepdog** (or "bobtail") is a bouncy, shaggy, waterproof dog that may be a cross between the bearded collie, the Hungarian puli, the Russian owtchar, and the French briard. Although called "old," the dog's ancestry goes back only about two hundred years.

A Great Pyrenees, which looks very much like one of the sheep,
guards its flock on a farm in Ellensburg, Washington.

Near the edge of a pasture, he noticed one of his dogs slowly
circling a ewe that had just given birth to a lamb. The next mo-
ment, a coyote slunk from behind a hillock, not 20 feet (6 meters)
away. It clearly had its eye on the newborn lamb.

Immediately, Jeff planted himself between the sheep and the coyote. He lowered his head threateningly. Jeff was about three times the coyote's size and could easily have chased or even killed the coyote. But all he did was bark a few times in warning. That was enough. The coyote turned and scooted away, its tail tucked between its hind legs.

"Good boy!" called the farmer, who had lost dozens of sheep to coyotes each year before Jeff came to help on the farm.

Jeff ambled off toward other sheep grazing nearby. He calmly looked back at the farmer as if to say "no big deal." To Jeff, scaring off a coyote is what a ranch guard is for.

**CHARACTERISTICS OF GUARDING DOGS** ▪ All guarding-dog breeds have strong protective instincts. Quiet-natured and slow-moving, they look lazy—until a strange animal or person comes near. Then what loud barking! One move from the stranger and the dog growls a warning, its ears flattened, its tail held high. Few intruders (except, perhaps, a grizzly bear or a cougar) care to argue with a big confident, threatening dog.

Not every guarding dog makes a perfect guard. Some roam off the farm. A few may chase sheep and sometimes even kill them. Some guard too well—and go after innocent people such as the veterinarian who comes to a farm to tend a sick animal. Some guarding dogs get in the way when a herding dog is at work—trying to protect the farm animals from another bossy dog. Most guarding dogs act as if they own the whole farm.

An Anatolian shepherd on guard in Minnesota to protect cattle from wolves and other intruders.

**THE WORK OF GUARDING DOGS** ▪ Depending on where they live, guarding dogs protect farm animals from wolves, foxes, bears, cougars, bobcats, human robbers, and especially coyotes and hungry dogs (wild or tame).

An Akbash on patrol. This dog can be aggressive and will
fight ferociously to protect its flock.

A guarding dog may spend its day resting in the shade with
one eye on a grazing flock. At night, it may trot around the pasture, checking the boundaries, scent-marking the territory with
its urine. Animal intruders take note of this smelly ''no trespass-
ing'' sign.

**TRAINING OF GUARDING DOGS** ▪ Guarding, patrolling, barking, and scent-marking instincts are so strong in guarding dogs

that the dogs need only be taught basic commands such as ''come'' and ''stay.''

Guarding dogs are not house dogs. On most farms they are brought up with the farm animals, not with people. The dogs and the animals they guard accept each other as ''family.'' On a sheep farm, a pup plays with the sheep as it would play with other dogs. (A komondor, with its woolly white coat, even looks like a sheep.)

The bond between this sheep and this Great Pyrenees developed as they grew up together on the farm. Each treats the other as part of its family.

Pups are taught not to play roughly. Some dogs have to be trained not to chase sheep in play. Expert trainers sometimes do this by attaching a long stick to the dog's collar for a few weeks. The stick only bothers the dog when it runs, and the dog soon gets the idea not to chase. (This is not, however, a good way to train a pet dog!)

An Anatolian shepherd puppy and friends. A pup that will be a sheep guarder needs to be raised with sheep, so that when the dog is grown it will naturally feel at home with its flock.

When a young dog starts working in the fields, it is often walked on leash around a pasture to show it where the boundaries are. Usually, at first, a dog is left alone with its herd for only a few hours at a time, then gradually longer. When the dog does take charge, it is watched closely, to make sure that it knows what to do. After that, ranch people visit it regularly, to see that it is well fed and healthy.

Both sheep and dog trust each other, and both know that the dog is in charge. Frightened sheep—or a ewe giving birth to a lamb—will sometimes go to the dog for protection. Besides scaring off predators, dogs seem to know instinctively when sheep are in trouble. A dog will go to a lamb caught in brambles. If a heavy-coated ewe falls over ("casts" herself) on her back, the dog will often pull on her neck wool to help her to her feet.

**HERDING AND GUARDING TRIALS** ▪ One hot, muggy day at a sheepdog trial (contest) in Maryland, a Border collie named Gail lazed in the shade beside a camper at the edge of a field. People were milling about. Scottish bagpipes were wailing in the distance. Other shepherds were shouting and whistling to their dogs.

Gail dozed, paying no attention to the commotion. But the minute Jim McEwen, her shepherd, called "Gail, come," she was on her feet. At a snap of Jim's fingers, she was off, her eye on five sheep at the end of the field. She headed toward them, running her "outrun" silently, steadily—in forty-four seconds. When she reached the far side of the sheep, Jim whistled. Gail dropped to the ground as if shot and caught the sheep's attention with her hypnotic ''eye.''

Gail got the sheep moving (''lifted'' them). Then, at Jim's thin, high whistled signal, she brought the sheep toward him (''fetched'' them). Dashing from side to side, she kept the sheep close as they went through a gate. As soon as the sheep reached Jim, he ordered Gail to take them back out into the field. This time she drove the sheep away from Jim, guiding them through a series of gates. At each gate, Gail had to dodge back and forth to keep the sheep together.

''Pushing five sheep through a gate,'' Jim muttered, ''is like trying to poke a marshmallow through a keyhole!''

As the sheep moved around, Jim kept calling and whistling to his dog, but Gail also made a lot of the moves on her own.

''She sometimes knows more than I do,'' Jim said. ''As close as Gail and I are, there's something between that dog and the sheep that's more than a person can understand.''

Next, Jim, with staff in hand, held open a gate, and Gail herded the five sheep into a pen. Her last test was to show that she could separate (''shed'' or ''shag'') one sheep from the others and hold it apart from the group.

''That'll do,'' Jim finally said. ''Good girl.''

Panting, Gail trotted over to a big tub of water. She jumped right into the tub, lapping up water as she cooled off. Hard work on a hot day! But not nearly so hard as an average day on the McEwen farm back in Dunkirk, Pennsylvania. The whole test had taken just ten minutes.

Jim McEwen and his dog Gail demonstrate their
skills at a sheepdog trial in Maryland.

Dozens of dog trials are held all over the world, where dogs
perform many of the jobs they do all year-round. Several breeds
take part in different kinds of competitions: herding, driving, and
guarding. Ducks, goats, cattle, or sheep are on hand to test the

Herding and guard dog competitions include various breeds such as Bearded collies and Old English sheepdogs, like the one shown here displaying speed, control—and style.

dogs' skills. Border collies are the stars of the sheepdog trials, and Gail often took home prizes. She did not win the trial that hot day in Maryland, but she had done her best. That was all Jim McEwen asked of his dog—who, on the job, could do the work of ten people.

And that is about all any shepherd can ask of any herding or guarding dog. Luckily, it is the nature of such dogs to be the bossiest bosses they can be.

# FURTHER READING

Ancona, George. *Sheep Dog.* New York: Lothrop, Lee & Shepherd, 1985.

Dudley, Ernest. *Scrap and Dog of the Storm.* North Yorkshire, England: Magna Print Books, 1979.

Fichter, George S. *Working Dogs.* New York: Watts, 1979.

Herriot, James. *Only One Woof.* New York: St. Martin's Press, 1985.

Lewis, Jean. *The Big Book of Dogs.* New York: Putnam, 1988.

Milon, Ellie. *201 Ways to Enjoy Your Dog.* Loveland, Colo.: Alpine Publications, 1990.

Patent, Dorothy. *Maggie, a Sheep Dog.* New York: Dodd, Mead, 1986.

Sanford, Bill and Carl Green. *Old English Sheepdog.* New York: Crestwood House, 1989.

# INDEX

# ABOUT THE AUTHOR

Freelance writer and editor Elizabeth Ring is a former teacher and an editor for *Ranger Rick* nature magazine. Her books for children include a picture book, *Night Flier,* and two biographies, *Rachel Carson: Caring for the Earth* and *Henry David Thoreau: In Step With Nature,* published by The Millbrook Press. Also published by The Millbrook Press are her other books in the *Good Dogs!* series. In addition, she has written on a range of programs on environmental subjects for the National Wildlife Federation. She lives in Woodbury, Connecticut, with her husband, writer and photographer William Hennefrund. Many dogs have been a part of the family over the years, but three cats and a German shepherd are current companions.